The Potential Trap
Why Focusing on Your "Full Potential" is Holding You Back (And What to Do Instead)

The Potential Trap

Psychology

Dr.Raam Harvard

Published by Poverty Eradication Trust (Triple ISO), 2025.

THE POTENTIAL TRAP

First edition. September 11, 2025.

ISBN: 978-9349611979

Written by Dr.Raam Harvard.

Also by Dr.Raam Harvard

Money

Demonetization the QUANTUM JUMP

DIGITAL Economy Millennium OPPORTUNITY

Psychology

What is Psychology?: Unlocking Practical Tools for Growth

The 7-Figure Network

The Potential Trap

Watch for more at https://drraam.com/.

Table of Contents

For the ones who were told they had limitless potential,

and have been running on empty ever since.

For the perfectionists, the overachievers, and the burnt-out dreamers

who did everything they were supposed to do,

only to feel like they're still not enough.

May you find permission in these pages to stop chasing,

and finally rest.

The thing that is really hard, and really amazing, is giving up on being perfect and beginning the work of becoming yourself.

— ANNA QUINDLEN

Introduction: The Catalyst Within You

Unleashing the Potential

In every individual lies a unique potential, a spark waiting to ignite the fires of change. Whether in personal endeavors or professional pursuits, the concept of being a catalyst encapsulates the essence of transformation. A catalyst is not merely a person; it is a force—an agent of change that accelerates progress and inspires action. The journey to unleash the catalyst within you is one of self-discovery, empowerment, and purposeful living.

As we navigate through life, we often encounter obstacles, doubts, and fears that can hinder our progress. Yet, it is essential to recognize that these challenges can serve as stepping stones to growth. Embracing the role of a catalyst means shifting your mindset from being a passive observer to an active participant in shaping your life and the lives of others. This book aims to guide you on that journey, providing the insights and tools needed to tap into your inherent potential.

Understanding the Catalyst Concept

Before we delve deeper, it's crucial to understand what being a catalyst truly means. In scientific terms, a catalyst is a substance that increases the rate of a chemical reaction without undergoing any permanent change itself. Analogously, in the realm of personal and professional development, a catalyst is someone who influences and accelerates change, fostering growth and innovation in themselves and others.

The concept of the catalyst extends beyond mere influence; it embodies the idea of creating a ripple effect—one small action leading to significant outcomes. Consider the story of Mahatma Gandhi, whose commitment to non-violent resistance and social change inspired millions across the globe. His actions catalyzed movements for civil rights and freedom, leaving an indelible mark on history. You, too, have the power to influence change in your sphere of life, sparking transformation that can resonate far beyond your immediate reach.

Personal and Organizational Impact

The impact of being a catalyst is multifaceted, influencing both personal and organizational realms. On a personal level, embracing the catalyst mindset fosters a sense of purpose and direction in life. It encourages individuals to pursue their passions, challenge the status quo, and take ownership of their decisions. This transformative approach can lead to increased fulfillment, self-awareness, and resilience.

In organizational contexts, catalysts play a pivotal role in driving innovation and change. They are the visionaries who identify opportunities for improvement, challenge existing paradigms, and inspire teams to embrace new approaches. For instance, in the tech industry, leaders like Steve Jobs and Elon Musk exemplified the catalyst mentality by pushing boundaries and redefining what was possible. Their relentless pursuit of innovation not only transformed their companies but also reshaped entire industries.

By recognizing the potential impact of becoming a catalyst, you can actively contribute to positive change in both your personal life and the organizations you are part of. This book will provide you with the frameworks and strategies to cultivate this mindset, empowering you to become a change agent in your own right.

Setting the Stage for Transformation

As we embark on this journey together, it is essential to establish a foundation for the transformative process that lies ahead. The chapters that follow will explore various dimensions of being a catalyst, from cultivating a transformative mindset to building meaningful relationships and taking decisive action.

1. Embracing Self-Discovery:

Understanding oneself is the first step in the catalyst journey. By exploring your values, strengths, and passions, you will gain clarity on your purpose and the unique contributions you can make to the world.

2. Cultivating a Transformative Mindset:

Your mindset plays a crucial role in shaping your actions and responses. We will delve into strategies for developing a growth mindset, overcoming self-doubt, and fostering resilience.

3. Setting Intentional Goals:

With a clear understanding of your purpose, you will learn how to set meaningful and intentional goals aligned with your values, creating a roadmap for your journey.

4. Building Meaningful Relationships:

Relationships are vital in the catalyst process. We will explore how to cultivate supportive connections and build a network of like-minded individuals who can inspire and empower you.

5. Taking Decisive Action:

Taking action is where transformation truly begins. We will discuss the importance of accountability and provide practical steps to help you move from intention to execution.

6. Navigating Challenges and Setbacks:

Every journey has its challenges. We will equip you with strategies to navigate obstacles, learn from setbacks, and maintain motivation through difficult times.

7. Celebrating Milestones:

Recognizing achievements, no matter how small, is essential for sustaining motivation. We will explore how to celebrate successes and maintain a sense of progress.

8. Fostering Continuous Growth:

The catalyst journey is not a destination but a lifelong pursuit. We will emphasize the importance of lifelong learning and embracing new opportunities for growth.

A Call to Action

As you read this book, I invite you to reflect on your own journey and consider the potential that lies within you. The catalyst within you is waiting to be unleashed—ready to spark change in your life and the lives of those around you. Embrace this opportunity for transformation, and prepare to embark on a journey that will revolutionize your path.

In conclusion, becoming a catalyst is not merely about creating change; it's about embodying the spirit of transformation. It requires courage, resilience, and a commitment to personal growth. As you delve into the chapters that follow, remember that you have the power to impact the world around you. The catalyst within you is not just a concept; it is a reality waiting to be realized.

Welcome to the journey of unleashing your inner catalyst—let's embark on this transformative adventure together!

Chapter 1: Embracing Self-Discovery

The Journey of Self-Discovery

Self-discovery is a transformative journey that involves introspection, reflection, and exploration of one's inner self. It is the process of understanding who you are, what you value, and what drives your passions. This journey is not just a one-time event; it is an ongoing process that can lead to profound changes in your life. Embracing self-discovery is the first essential step toward becoming a catalyst for change in your own life and in the lives of others.

Why Self-Discovery Matters

Understanding yourself is crucial for several reasons:

1. **Clarity of Purpose:** Knowing your values, strengths, and passions provides clarity on what you want to achieve in life. It helps you set meaningful goals that align with your authentic self.
2. **Informed Decision-Making:** When you have a clear understanding of who you are, you are better equipped to make decisions that resonate with your true self, leading to greater satisfaction and fulfillment.
3. **Resilience in Challenges:** Self-awareness fosters resilience. Understanding your strengths and weaknesses allows you to navigate challenges more effectively and maintain motivation during difficult times.
4. **Enhanced Relationships:** The more you know about yourself, the better you can communicate your needs and boundaries to others. This fosters healthier and more meaningful relationships.

Key Components of Self-Discovery

Self-discovery involves three key components: values, strengths, and passions. Let's explore each of these components in detail.

1. Identifying Your Values

Values are the core beliefs that guide your actions and decisions. They reflect what is most important to you and serve as a compass for your life. Identifying your values is crucial for living authentically and making choices that align with your true self.

Exercise: Values Assessment

Take a moment to reflect on the values that resonate with you. Here's a simple exercise to help you identify your core values:

- **Step 1:** List the top ten values that matter most to you. Examples might include honesty, integrity, family, creativity, or personal growth.

- **Step 2:** Rank these values in order of importance to you.
- **Step 3:** Select your top three values. Write them down and reflect on why they are significant to you.

Understanding your values will help you align your goals and decisions with what truly matters in your life.

2. Recognizing Your Strengths

Strengths are the skills and attributes that you naturally possess. They are the qualities that set you apart and contribute to your success. Recognizing your strengths is essential for building confidence and leveraging your unique abilities to make a difference.

Exercise: Strengths Inventory

To identify your strengths, consider the following steps:

- **Step 1:** Reflect on your past achievements. What skills did you use to accomplish them? Write down at least five accomplishments and the strengths you demonstrated.
- **Step 2:** Ask for feedback from trusted friends, family, or colleagues. What do they perceive as your strengths? Create a list based on their feedback.
- **Step 3:** Review your list of strengths and select the top three that you believe define you. Write them down and consider how you can utilize these strengths in your personal and professional life.

Recognizing your strengths will empower you to embrace who you are and use your unique abilities to create meaningful impact.

3. Discovering Your Passions

Passions are the activities, interests, and pursuits that excite and energize you. They are the things that make you feel alive and fulfilled. Discovering your passions is key to living a purpose-driven life.

Exercise: Passion Exploration

To explore your passions, follow these steps:

- **Step 1:** Think about activities that bring you joy. What do you love to do in your free time? Create a list of activities that make you feel fulfilled.
- **Step 2:** Reflect on moments when you lost track of time because you were so engaged in an activity. What were you doing? Write down these experiences.
- **Step 3:** Identify any common themes or interests in your lists. What passions emerge? Choose the top three passions that resonate with you.

Discovering your passions will guide you toward pursuits that align with your values and strengths, fueling your journey as a catalyst.

The Interconnection of Values, Strengths, and Passions

The interplay between your values, strengths, and passions creates a powerful foundation for your journey of self-discovery. When these three elements align, you can craft a life that is authentic, meaningful, and impactful. For instance, if your top value is personal growth, your strength is effective communication, and your passion is mentoring others, you can create opportunities to lead workshops or coach individuals.

Overcoming Obstacles to Self-Discovery

While the journey of self-discovery is empowering, it can also present challenges. Many individuals face obstacles such as self-doubt, fear of judgment, and societal expectations that may cloud their understanding of who they are. Here are some strategies to overcome these obstacles:

1. **Practice Self-Compassion:** Be kind to yourself throughout this journey. Understand that self-discovery takes time, and it's okay to feel uncertain or lost at times.
2. **Challenge Limiting Beliefs:** Identify any beliefs that hold you back from embracing your true self. Challenge these beliefs and

replace them with affirmations that empower you.

3. **Create a Safe Space for Reflection:** Set aside time for quiet reflection. Whether through journaling, meditation, or walks in nature, create an environment that fosters introspection.
4. **Seek Support:** Surround yourself with supportive individuals who encourage your journey. Share your aspirations and challenges with trusted friends or mentors.

The Role of Reflection in Self-Discovery

Reflection is a powerful tool in the self-discovery process. It allows you to pause, assess your experiences, and gain insights into your thoughts and feelings. Regular reflection can deepen your understanding of yourself and enhance your ability to make informed choices.

Exercise: Reflection Journal

To cultivate a habit of reflection, consider keeping a reflection journal. Here's how to get started:

- **Step 1:** Set aside time each week to reflect on your experiences, thoughts, and feelings.
- **Step 2:** Write freely about what you learned during the week. What challenges did you face? What successes did you achieve? What insights did you gain?
- **Step 3:** Review your journal entries regularly. Look for patterns, recurring themes, and personal growth.

Journaling can help you track your progress and reinforce the lessons learned on your journey of self-discovery.

Integrating Self-Discovery into Daily Life

As you embark on your self-discovery journey, it's essential to integrate your newfound insights into your daily life. Here are some practical strategies to help you do so:

1. **Set Intentional Goals:** Based on your values, strengths, and passions, set specific and actionable goals that align with your authentic self. Create a plan to work toward these goals.
2. **Cultivate Mindfulness:** Practice mindfulness techniques to stay present and connected to your thoughts and feelings. Mindfulness can enhance self-awareness and help you make conscious choices.
3. **Seek Opportunities for Growth:** Embrace new experiences that align with your passions. Attend workshops, join clubs, or volunteer in areas that excite you.
4. **Review and Adjust:** Regularly revisit your values, strengths, and passions. As you grow and evolve, your insights may change, so be open to adjusting your goals and pursuits accordingly.

Conclusion: Embracing Your Authentic Self

The journey of self-discovery is a lifelong process that requires commitment, curiosity, and self-compassion. By embracing self-discovery, you empower yourself to become the catalyst of change in your life and in the lives of others. Remember that understanding your values, strengths, and passions is not just about personal growth; it is about creating a ripple effect of positive change in your community and beyond.

As you continue your journey, hold onto the insights gained from this chapter and use them as a foundation for the transformative work that lies ahead. By embracing your authentic self, you will not only inspire yourself but also inspire those around you to do the same. Welcome to the adventure of self-discovery—your journey has just begun!

Chapter 2: Cultivating a Transformative Mindset

The Transformative Mindset

A transformative mindset is the cornerstone of personal and professional growth. It allows individuals to view challenges as opportunities for learning and development rather than insurmountable obstacles. This chapter will delve into the concept of a growth mindset, highlight the significance of resilience and adaptability, and provide practical techniques to help you cultivate a transformative mindset.

Understanding the Growth Mindset

The term "growth mindset" was popularized by psychologist Carol Dweck, who describes it as the belief that abilities and intelligence can be developed through dedication, hard work, and perseverance. In contrast, a fixed mindset is the belief that talents and intelligence are static traits that cannot change.

Key Characteristics of a Growth Mindset

1. **Embracing Challenges:** Individuals with a growth mindset see challenges as opportunities for growth rather than threats to their abilities.
2. **Persistence in the Face of Setbacks:** Those with a growth mindset view failures as learning experiences and are more likely to persist when faced with obstacles.
3. **Value of Effort:** A growth mindset emphasizes the importance of effort and hard work in achieving success, understanding that mastery comes from dedication.
4. **Learning from Criticism:** Constructive feedback is seen as a valuable tool for improvement, leading to continuous self-development.
5. **Inspired by Others' Success:** Instead of feeling threatened by the success of others, individuals with a growth mindset celebrate it and use it as inspiration for their own growth.

The Importance of a Growth Mindset

Cultivating a growth mindset is essential for several reasons:

1. **Enhanced Learning:** A growth mindset promotes a love of learning, encouraging individuals to seek new knowledge and skills.
2. **Increased Resilience:** Individuals with a growth mindset are better equipped to handle adversity, bounce back from setbacks, and maintain motivation in challenging situations.

3. **Improved Performance:** Research has shown that those with a growth mindset tend to achieve higher levels of performance, as they are more likely to take risks and push beyond their comfort zones.
4. **Greater Adaptability:** In an ever-changing world, adaptability is crucial. A growth mindset allows individuals to adjust to new circumstances and embrace change.

Overcoming Limiting Beliefs

Limiting beliefs are the negative thoughts and assumptions we hold about ourselves and our abilities. These beliefs can hinder personal growth and prevent us from reaching our full potential. To cultivate a transformative mindset, it is crucial to identify and overcome these limiting beliefs.

Common Limiting Beliefs

1. **"I'm Not Good Enough."** This belief stems from comparing oneself to others or past failures.
2. **"I Can't Change."** Some individuals feel trapped in their current circumstances, believing that change is impossible.
3. **"Failure Is Bad."** The fear of failure can prevent individuals from taking risks and pursuing their goals.
4. **"I Don't Have What It Takes."** This belief can arise from feelings of inadequacy or a lack of confidence in one's abilities.

Strategies for Overcoming Limiting Beliefs

1. **Identify Your Limiting Beliefs:** Start by reflecting on the negative thoughts that arise when you face challenges. Write down these beliefs to gain clarity.
2. **Challenge the Validity of Your Beliefs:** Ask yourself if these beliefs are based on facts or assumptions. Are they helping or

hindering your growth? Counter them with evidence of your successes and capabilities.

3. **Reframe Your Perspective:** Instead of viewing challenges as threats, see them as opportunities for growth. Reframe your self-talk to emphasize possibilities rather than limitations. For example, change "I can't do this" to "I can learn how to do this."
4. **Practice Positive Affirmations:** Use affirmations to reinforce a positive self-image. Repeat statements such as "I am capable of growth" or "I embrace challenges as opportunities" daily.
5. **Surround Yourself with Positive Influences:** Seek out individuals who embody a growth mindset. Their encouragement and perspectives can inspire you to challenge your limiting beliefs.

Building Resilience

Resilience is the ability to bounce back from adversity, maintain a positive attitude, and continue moving forward. Cultivating resilience is vital for navigating life's challenges and setbacks.

Key Components of Resilience

1. **Emotional Awareness:** Understanding your emotions and how they impact your thoughts and actions is essential for resilience. Being aware of your feelings allows you to respond effectively to challenges.
2. **Optimism:** Maintaining a hopeful outlook can enhance resilience. Optimistic individuals are more likely to see setbacks as temporary and manageable.
3. **Social Support:** Building a network of supportive relationships provides encouragement and perspective during tough times.
4. **Problem-Solving Skills:** The ability to identify solutions and

take action in the face of challenges fosters resilience.

Techniques to Develop Resilience

1. **Practice Mindfulness:** Mindfulness techniques, such as meditation or deep breathing, can help you stay grounded and manage stress. These practices foster emotional awareness and allow you to respond thoughtfully to challenges.
2. **Develop a Support System:** Surround yourself with positive influences and supportive individuals. Share your struggles with trusted friends or mentors who can provide encouragement and guidance.
3. **Set Realistic Goals:** Break larger goals into smaller, achievable steps. This approach helps you maintain motivation and celebrate progress along the way.
4. **Embrace Change:** Instead of resisting change, learn to adapt and embrace new circumstances. View change as an opportunity for growth rather than a threat.
5. **Reflect on Past Resilience:** Recall previous challenges you have overcome and the skills you used to navigate them. Recognizing your resilience can empower you to face future obstacles with confidence.

Cultivating Adaptability

Adaptability is the ability to adjust to new situations and respond effectively to change. In today's fast-paced world, being adaptable is crucial for success.

The Importance of Adaptability

1. **Navigating Uncertainty:** Adaptability allows individuals to thrive in uncertain environments by being open to new possibilities and approaches.

2. **Enhancing Problem-Solving:** Adaptive individuals can think creatively and find innovative solutions to challenges.
3. **Maintaining Well-Being:** Flexibility in thinking and behavior can reduce stress and promote mental well-being, as adaptable individuals are less likely to become overwhelmed by change.

Strategies to Enhance Adaptability

1. **Embrace a Learning Mindset:** Approach new experiences with curiosity and a willingness to learn. Be open to feedback and seek opportunities for growth.
2. **Experiment and Take Risks:** Step out of your comfort zone by trying new things. Embrace the possibility of failure as a valuable part of the learning process.
3. **Stay Informed:** Keep up with trends and changes in your personal and professional life. Being informed allows you to anticipate changes and adapt proactively.
4. **Practice Flexibility:** Cultivate the ability to adjust your plans and strategies as circumstances change. Being open to alternatives fosters adaptability.
5. **Seek Diverse Perspectives:** Engage with individuals from different backgrounds and experiences. Diverse perspectives can broaden your understanding and enhance your adaptability in various situations.

Conclusion: The Power of a Transformative Mindset

Cultivating a transformative mindset is an essential step toward becoming a catalyst for change. By embracing a growth mindset, overcoming limiting beliefs, and developing resilience and adaptability, you empower yourself to navigate challenges and seize opportunities.

As you continue on your journey, remember that cultivating a transformative mindset is a lifelong process. Practice the techniques discussed in this chapter, and be patient with yourself as you grow and evolve. By embracing your potential for transformation, you can inspire not only yourself but also those around you to embark on their own journeys of change.

Chapter 3: Setting Intentional Goals

Intentional Goals

Setting intentional goals is a transformative process that empowers individuals to align their aspirations with their core values and passions. Unlike arbitrary goals that may lead to fleeting motivation, intentional goals are deeply connected to who you are and what you want to achieve. This chapter will guide you through the process of establishing meaningful goals and offer frameworks for creating a compelling vision for your future.

Understanding the Importance of Intentional Goals

Intentional goals serve as a roadmap for your personal and professional journey. They help you clarify your desires and aspirations, guiding your decisions and actions. Here are some key reasons why setting intentional goals is vital:

1. **Clarity of Purpose:** Intentional goals provide clarity about what you want to achieve and why it matters. This clarity enables you to focus your energy and resources on what truly matters to you.
2. **Alignment with Values:** Goals that align with your values create a sense of fulfillment and purpose. When your goals reflect your core beliefs, you are more likely to stay motivated and committed to achieving them.
3. **Increased Motivation:** Intentional goals evoke a sense of excitement and inspiration, driving you to take action. When you set goals that resonate with your values, you are more likely to remain engaged and motivated.
4. **Enhanced Decision-Making:** With a clear set of intentional goals, you can make better decisions. When faced with choices, you can evaluate options based on whether they align with your goals, simplifying the decision-making process.
5. **Accountability and Focus:** Setting intentional goals fosters a sense of accountability. By defining what you want to achieve, you create a framework for measuring progress and holding yourself accountable for your actions.

The Goal-Setting Process

Setting intentional goals involves a systematic approach that incorporates self-reflection, planning, and action. The following steps outline a comprehensive goal-setting process:

1. Self-Reflection

Before setting goals, it's essential to engage in self-reflection to gain a deeper understanding of your values, strengths, and aspirations. Consider the following questions:

- What are my core values? (e.g., family, career, health, creativity)
- What passions and interests bring me joy?
- What accomplishments am I most proud of, and what did I learn from them?
- What challenges have I faced, and how have they shaped my perspective?
- How do I define success in my life?

Taking the time to reflect on these questions will help you identify what truly matters to you and inform your goal-setting process.

2. Identifying Your Goals

Once you have clarity about your values and aspirations, it's time to identify specific goals that align with them. To create intentional goals, use the SMART criteria, which stands for:

- **Specific:** Define your goals clearly and concisely. Instead of saying, "I want to get fit," specify, "I want to run a 5K in under 30 minutes."
- **Measurable:** Establish criteria for measuring your progress. This will help you stay on track and motivated. For example, "I will work out three times a week."
- **Achievable:** Ensure your goals are realistic and attainable. Setting overly ambitious goals can lead to frustration. Assess your current situation and capabilities to determine what is feasible.
- **Relevant:** Your goals should be relevant to your values and aspirations. They should resonate with who you are and what you want to achieve in life.
- **Time-bound:** Set a deadline for your goals to create a sense of urgency and accountability. For instance, "I will complete my 5K training by March 1st."

3. Creating a Compelling Vision

A compelling vision serves as the foundation for your intentional goals. It paints a vivid picture of your desired future, helping you stay motivated and focused on your journey. To create a compelling vision, follow these steps:

1. **Visualize Your Future:** Take some time to envision what your ideal life looks like. Imagine your career, relationships, health, and personal growth. Consider writing a detailed description of this vision, focusing on how it feels and what it looks like.
2. **Create a Vision Board:** A vision board is a visual representation of your goals and aspirations. Gather images, quotes, and symbols that resonate with your vision, and arrange them on a board or digital platform. Place your vision board in a prominent location to remind you of your goals daily.
3. **Craft a Vision Statement:** Write a concise vision statement that encapsulates your aspirations. This statement should reflect your values and what you want to achieve in the long term. For example, "I envision a fulfilling career where I inspire others through my work and create positive change in my community."

Aligning Goals with Values

Aligning your goals with your core values is crucial for maintaining motivation and fulfillment throughout your journey. Consider the following strategies for ensuring alignment:

1. **Prioritize Your Values:** Identify your top three to five core values. Use these values as a guide when setting goals. For instance, if family is a core value, consider how your goals may impact your family life.

2. **Evaluate Goals Against Values:** Regularly assess your goals to ensure they align with your values. If you find discrepancies, adjust your goals accordingly. This process helps you stay true to yourself and fosters a sense of integrity.
3. **Celebrate Values-Driven Achievements:** Acknowledge and celebrate achievements that reflect your values. Recognizing progress in areas that matter to you reinforces the importance of staying aligned with your core beliefs.

Overcoming Challenges in Goal Setting

While setting intentional goals is empowering, challenges may arise along the way. Here are common obstacles and strategies for overcoming them:

1. **Fear of Failure:** Fear of failure can hinder goal-setting and progress. Embrace failure as a valuable learning opportunity and a natural part of the journey. Shift your mindset to view setbacks as stepping stones to success.
2. **Lack of Motivation:** At times, motivation may wane. To reignite your motivation, revisit your vision and remind yourself of the reasons behind your goals. Surround yourself with supportive individuals who inspire and uplift you.
3. **Overwhelm:** Setting too many goals at once can lead to feelings of overwhelm. Focus on a few key goals at a time and break them into smaller, manageable steps. This approach allows you to make consistent progress without feeling overwhelmed.
4. **External Distractions:** Life is full of distractions that can derail your focus. Create a conducive environment for goal achievement by minimizing distractions. Establish routines and time blocks dedicated to working on your goals.

Accountability and Support

Establishing accountability and seeking support can significantly enhance your goal-setting journey. Here are ways to foster accountability and build a support network:

1. **Share Your Goals:** Share your goals with trusted friends, family, or mentors. By vocalizing your aspirations, you create a sense of accountability. Encourage them to check in on your progress and offer support.
2. **Join a Support Group:** Consider joining a group or community focused on personal development or goal achievement. Engaging with like-minded individuals provides encouragement, accountability, and valuable insights.
3. **Track Your Progress:** Regularly track your progress toward your goals. Use journals, apps, or spreadsheets to record milestones and reflect on your journey. Celebrate your achievements, no matter how small.

Creating an Action Plan

An action plan is a detailed roadmap outlining the steps needed to achieve your goals. To create an effective action plan, follow these steps:

1. **Break Down Goals into Actionable Steps:** Divide each goal into smaller, actionable tasks. This breakdown makes the goals feel more manageable and allows for steady progress.
2. **Set Deadlines for Each Task:** Assign deadlines to each task to maintain momentum and accountability. Having a timeline helps you stay focused and organized.
3. **Identify Resources and Support:** Determine the resources you need to achieve your goals. This could include books, courses, mentors, or tools. Additionally, identify individuals who can provide support along the way.

4. **Review and Adjust Regularly:** Periodically review your action plan to assess progress and make adjustments as needed. Flexibility is key to adapting to changes and staying aligned with your goals.

Conclusion: The Journey of Intentional Goal Setting

Setting intentional goals is a transformative journey that empowers you to align your aspirations with your values and passions. By engaging in self-reflection, creating a compelling vision, and overcoming challenges, you can cultivate a powerful framework for achieving your dreams.

As you embark on this journey, remember that goal setting is not a one-time event but an ongoing process of growth and evolution. Embrace the journey, celebrate your achievements, and remain open to new possibilities as you pursue a future that reflects your true self.

Chapter 4: Building Meaningful Relationships

Importance of Relationships

Human beings are inherently social creatures. Our relationships profoundly influence our lives, shaping our experiences, decisions, and personal growth. Building meaningful relationships is crucial for our emotional well-being and professional success. In this chapter, we will explore the importance of relationships in personal growth and discuss strategies for effective networking, collaboration, and seeking mentorship to foster a supportive community.

The Role of Relationships in Personal Growth

1. **Emotional Support:** Meaningful relationships provide emotional support during challenging times. Friends, family, and mentors can offer encouragement, understanding, and guidance, helping us navigate difficulties and build resilience.
2. **Personal Development:** Relationships challenge us to grow and evolve. They expose us to diverse perspectives, ideas, and experiences, encouraging us to step outside our comfort zones and expand our horizons.
3. **Increased Motivation:** Surrounding ourselves with supportive individuals can enhance motivation and drive. When we share our goals with others, their encouragement can inspire us to stay committed and accountable.
4. **Opportunities for Learning:** Relationships create opportunities for learning and skill development. Collaborating with others allows us to gain new insights, learn from their experiences, and develop new competencies.
5. **Networking and Career Advancement:** In the professional realm, relationships play a pivotal role in career advancement. Networking and building connections can lead to new opportunities, collaborations, and mentorship that can propel us forward.

Understanding Different Types of Relationships

To build meaningful relationships, it's essential to recognize the various types of connections we can cultivate:

1. **Personal Relationships:** These include friendships, family connections, and romantic partnerships. Personal relationships provide emotional support and companionship, enriching our lives.
2. **Professional Relationships:** These encompass colleagues, mentors, and industry connections. Professional relationships

facilitate networking, collaboration, and career advancement.

3. **Community Connections:** Engaging with community groups, organizations, and volunteer networks fosters a sense of belonging and shared purpose, creating meaningful connections with like-minded individuals.
4. **Mentorship Relationships:** Mentors provide guidance, support, and wisdom based on their experiences. Building mentorship relationships can significantly impact personal and professional development.

Strategies for Building Meaningful Relationships

1. Effective Networking

Networking is about creating authentic connections rather than merely exchanging contact information. Here are strategies for effective networking:

- **Be Genuine:** Approach networking with authenticity. Show genuine interest in others and seek to understand their experiences and perspectives.
- **Attend Events:** Participate in conferences, workshops, and networking events relevant to your interests or profession. These gatherings provide opportunities to meet new people and establish connections.
- **Utilize Social Media:** Platforms like LinkedIn, Twitter, and Facebook can facilitate networking. Engage with others in your field by commenting on their posts, sharing insights, and initiating conversations.
- **Follow Up:** After meeting someone, send a follow-up message to express your appreciation for the conversation. This gesture reinforces your interest and lays the groundwork for further communication.
- **Offer Value:** Networking is a two-way street. Consider how

you can offer value to others in your network. Share relevant resources, insights, or connections that can benefit them.

2. Cultivating Collaborative Relationships

Collaboration is a powerful way to build meaningful relationships. Here's how to foster collaborative connections:

- **Identify Common Goals:** Look for opportunities to collaborate with others who share similar goals or values. Identify projects or initiatives where your skills and expertise can complement each other.
- **Communicate Openly:** Effective communication is key to successful collaboration. Be open and transparent about your expectations, ideas, and feedback throughout the process.
- **Celebrate Collective Success:** Acknowledge and celebrate the achievements of the group, not just individual accomplishments. Recognizing collective success fosters a sense of camaraderie and strengthens relationships.
- **Be Respectful and Supportive:** Treat collaborators with respect and support. Appreciate their contributions and be willing to offer help when needed.

3. Seeking Mentorship

Mentorship is a valuable relationship that can significantly impact personal and professional growth. Here's how to seek out and build mentorship relationships:

- **Identify Potential Mentors:** Look for individuals who inspire you and possess the qualities or experiences you aspire to. These could be professionals in your field, teachers, or community leaders.
- **Reach Out:** When approaching potential mentors, be clear

about your intentions. Share your goals and explain why you value their guidance. A well-crafted message can make a positive impression.

- **Be Respectful of Their Time:** Recognize that mentors are often busy individuals. Be mindful of their time and schedule meetings or calls that accommodate their availability.
- **Be Open to Feedback:** Mentorship is a learning opportunity. Be open to receiving feedback and guidance from your mentor. Approach the relationship with a growth mindset and a willingness to learn.
- **Show Gratitude:** Express gratitude for your mentor's time and support. A simple thank-you note or message can strengthen the relationship and show your appreciation.

Building a Supportive Community

Creating a supportive community is essential for personal growth. Here's how to foster a community that encourages connection and collaboration:

1. **Join Interest-Based Groups:** Seek out groups or organizations that align with your interests, values, or goals. Engaging with like-minded individuals fosters connection and shared experiences.
2. **Participate in Volunteer Opportunities:** Volunteering in your community allows you to meet new people and contribute to meaningful causes. Shared experiences in service create bonds and deepen relationships.
3. **Host Gatherings:** Organize events, meetups, or workshops to bring people together. Creating spaces for connection fosters community and encourages collaboration.
4. **Be an Active Contributor:** Actively participate in community discussions, forums, or online groups. Share your insights,

experiences, and resources, contributing to a culture of support and growth.

Overcoming Challenges in Building Relationships

While building meaningful relationships is rewarding, challenges may arise. Here are strategies for overcoming common obstacles:

1. **Fear of Rejection:** Fear of rejection can hinder relationship-building efforts. Recognize that not everyone will respond positively, and that's okay. Focus on building connections with those who resonate with you.
2. **Time Constraints:** Busy schedules can make it challenging to nurture relationships. Prioritize relationship-building by setting aside dedicated time for networking, collaboration, and mentorship.
3. **Miscommunication:** Miscommunication can lead to misunderstandings in relationships. Practice active listening and clarify expectations to avoid potential conflicts.
4. **Maintaining Boundaries:** While fostering relationships is essential, it's also important to establish boundaries. Ensure that relationships are mutually beneficial and respectful of each person's time and energy.

Conclusion: The Power of Meaningful Relationships

Building meaningful relationships is a transformative journey that enriches our lives and supports personal growth. By prioritizing connections, cultivating collaboration, and seeking mentorship, we create a supportive community that empowers us to thrive.

As you continue on your journey, remember that the quality of your relationships directly influences your overall well-being and success. Embrace the power of meaningful connections, and take proactive steps to nurture and expand your network. Together, we can create a world where individuals uplift and support one another, fostering a sense of belonging and collective growth.

Chapter 5: Taking Decisive Action

Introduction to Decisive Action

Taking action is the cornerstone of transformation and personal growth. While self-discovery, mindset, and relationships are crucial for laying the groundwork, the true catalyst for change lies in our ability to act decisively. In this chapter, we will explore the significance of taking action, the role of accountability in achieving our goals, and provide actionable steps, tools, and systems to help readers move from intention to execution.

The Importance of Taking Action

1. **Turning Intentions into Reality:** Many individuals possess

great ideas and aspirations but fail to act upon them. Action is what bridges the gap between intention and reality. It is the catalyst that turns dreams into achievable outcomes.

2. **Building Momentum:** Taking decisive action creates momentum. The more we act, the more motivated we become, leading to a positive cycle of achievement. Small steps can lead to significant changes over time.
3. **Gaining Experience and Confidence:** Action fosters learning and growth. Each step we take provides valuable experience, helping us refine our skills and build confidence in our abilities.
4. **Overcoming Fear and Procrastination:** Fear of failure or perfectionism often leads to procrastination. Taking action, even in small increments, helps us confront these fears and move beyond them.
5. **Creating Opportunities:** Action opens doors to new opportunities. By taking steps toward our goals, we increase our visibility, expand our networks, and position ourselves for success.

The Role of Accountability

Accountability is a powerful force that enhances our commitment to taking action. Here's how accountability plays a crucial role in achieving our goals:

1. **Motivation and Commitment:** Sharing our goals with others creates a sense of accountability. Knowing that someone else is aware of our intentions motivates us to follow through.
2. **Feedback and Support:** Accountability partners or groups provide valuable feedback and support. They help us stay on track, offer encouragement, and hold us accountable for our commitments.
3. **Goal Setting and Progress Tracking:** Establishing specific

goals with measurable outcomes encourages accountability. Regular check-ins with an accountability partner help us assess our progress and make necessary adjustments.

4. **Creating a Supportive Environment:** Being part of an accountability group fosters a supportive environment where individuals can share challenges, celebrate successes, and motivate each other.

Taking Action: Steps to Move from Intention to Execution

1. Define Clear Goals

- **Be Specific:** Clearly articulate what you want to achieve. Specificity helps eliminate ambiguity and provides a clear target to aim for.
- **Set Measurable Outcomes:** Establish metrics to measure your progress. This could include deadlines, numerical targets, or specific milestones that signify achievement.
- **Ensure Relevance:** Ensure your goals align with your values and aspirations. Relevant goals are more likely to motivate action and sustain commitment.
- **Time-Bound:** Set realistic deadlines for achieving your goals. A timeline creates a sense of urgency and encourages prompt action.

2. Break Goals into Actionable Steps

- **Chunking:** Divide larger goals into smaller, manageable tasks. Breaking goals into actionable steps makes them less overwhelming and more achievable.
- **Create a Task List:** Write down the specific actions required to accomplish each step. This serves as a roadmap for your

journey and helps maintain focus.

- **Prioritize Tasks:** Identify which tasks are most critical and prioritize them. Focusing on high-impact actions can accelerate your progress.

3. Develop a Plan of Action

- **Create a Timeline:** Establish a timeline for completing each task. This helps you stay organized and accountable for your progress.
- **Identify Resources:** Determine what resources (tools, information, support) you need to execute your plan effectively.
- **Anticipate Challenges:** Identify potential obstacles and develop strategies for overcoming them. This proactive approach prepares you to tackle challenges head-on.

4. Implement Tools and Systems for Execution

- **Task Management Tools:** Utilize digital tools such as Trello, Asana, or Todoist to organize and track your tasks. These platforms help streamline your workflow and ensure accountability.
- **Habit-Tracking Apps:** Consider using habit-tracking apps to monitor daily actions related to your goals. These apps provide visual reminders of your progress and reinforce positive habits.
- **Time-Blocking:** Use time-blocking techniques to allocate specific time slots for focused work on your tasks. This strategy minimizes distractions and enhances productivity.
- **Create Routines:** Establish daily or weekly routines that include dedicated time for working on your goals. Consistent routines promote discipline and accountability.

5. Establish Accountability Mechanisms

- **Find an Accountability Partner:** Partner with someone who shares similar goals or interests. Regular check-ins will help keep you both motivated and on track.
- **Join an Accountability Group:** Consider joining or forming a group where members can share their goals, progress, and challenges. The group dynamic fosters mutual support and accountability.
- **Regular Progress Reviews:** Schedule regular reviews of your progress. Reflect on what worked, what didn't, and adjust your approach as needed.
- **Celebrate Milestones:** Acknowledge and celebrate your achievements, no matter how small. Celebrating milestones reinforces positive behavior and motivates further action.

Overcoming Obstacles to Action

Despite the best intentions, obstacles may arise that hinder our ability to take action. Here are strategies for overcoming common barriers:

1. **Fear of Failure:** Acknowledge that failure is a part of the learning process. Reframe failure as an opportunity for growth and a stepping stone to success.
2. **Perfectionism:** Let go of the need for perfection. Focus on progress rather than perfection, and embrace the idea that taking imperfect action is better than inaction.
3. **Lack of Motivation:** Revisit your "why" – the deeper reasons behind your goals. Connecting with your intrinsic motivations can reignite your drive to take action.
4. **Distractions:** Identify distractions that impede your focus. Create an environment conducive to productivity by minimizing interruptions and setting boundaries.

5. **Overwhelm:** If you feel overwhelmed, return to the practice of chunking tasks. Focus on one small step at a time to regain a sense of control and progress.

Conclusion: The Power of Decisive Action

Taking decisive action is the catalyst that transforms intentions into tangible results. By understanding the importance of action, embracing accountability, and implementing practical strategies, readers can overcome obstacles and achieve their goals.

As you move forward on your journey, remember that action is not just about making big leaps; it's about the small, consistent steps that lead to meaningful change. Embrace the power of decisive action, and trust that each step you take brings you closer to your aspirations.

Chapter 6: Navigating Challenges and Setbacks

Embracing the Journey

Every journey toward transformation and personal growth is fraught with challenges and setbacks. While the excitement of setting goals and taking action propels us forward, the reality is that obstacles will arise. This chapter prepares readers to face those challenges head-on, equipping them with insights on resilience, problem-solving, and maintaining motivation during tough times. By understanding that setbacks are a natural part of the process, readers can cultivate the mindset and skills needed to navigate difficulties and continue their journey with determination.

The Nature of Challenges and Setbacks

1. **Inevitability of Challenges:** Challenges are an inherent part of any worthwhile pursuit. Whether they stem from external circumstances or internal doubts, setbacks will occur. Acknowledging their inevitability is the first step toward resilience.
2. **Types of Setbacks:** Setbacks can manifest in various forms, including:
    - **External Setbacks:** Economic downturns, unexpected events, or obstacles beyond one's control.
    - **Internal Setbacks:** Self-doubt, fear of failure, or loss of motivation that can derail progress.
    - **Interpersonal Challenges:** Conflicts with colleagues, friends, or mentors that may create barriers.
3. **The Role of Mindset:** Our mindset significantly influences how we respond to challenges. Adopting a growth mindset can help individuals view setbacks as opportunities for learning and growth rather than insurmountable obstacles.

Building Resilience

Resilience is the ability to bounce back from adversity and continue pursuing one's goals. Here are key strategies to foster resilience:

1. **Developing a Resilient Mindset:**
    - **Reframe Challenges:** Encourage readers to reframe setbacks as learning experiences. Instead of viewing failure as a dead end, they should see it as a stepping stone toward growth.
    - **Practice Self-Compassion:** Self-compassion involves

treating oneself with kindness during difficult times. Readers should learn to forgive themselves for mistakes and recognize that everyone faces setbacks.

2. **Strengthening Emotional Resilience:**
    - **Emotional Awareness:** Encourage readers to acknowledge and process their emotions. Understanding feelings such as frustration or disappointment can help them navigate challenges more effectively.
    - **Building a Support System:** Surrounding oneself with supportive friends, family, or mentors provides a buffer against setbacks. Encouragement from others can help maintain motivation.
3. **Creating a Resilience Toolkit:**
    - **Mindfulness and Stress Management:** Techniques such as mindfulness meditation, deep breathing, or yoga can help manage stress and enhance emotional resilience.
    - **Physical Well-Being:** Regular exercise, a balanced diet, and sufficient sleep are crucial for maintaining mental and emotional health. Encourage readers to prioritize self-care during tough times.

Problem-Solving Strategies

When faced with challenges, effective problem-solving skills are essential. Here's how readers can develop their problem-solving abilities:

1. **Identify the Problem:**
    - **Clarify the Issue:** Encourage readers to define the specific challenge they are facing. A clear understanding of the problem allows for more

effective solutions.
   - **Gather Information:** Collect relevant information about the issue. This may involve seeking feedback from others or conducting research.
2. **Explore Possible Solutions:**
   - **Brainstorming:** Encourage creative brainstorming sessions to generate potential solutions. Readers should aim for quantity over quality at this stage to explore all possibilities.
   - **Consider Alternatives:** Evaluate different approaches and alternatives. Discuss the pros and cons of each solution.
3. **Take Action:**
   - **Select a Solution:** Choose the most viable solution based on the analysis. Encourage readers to trust their instincts while being open to adjustments.
   - **Implement and Monitor:** Take decisive action to implement the chosen solution. Monitor progress and remain flexible to adapt as needed.
4. **Learn from the Experience:**
   - **Reflect on the Outcome:** After navigating a challenge, encourage readers to reflect on the process. What worked well? What could be improved for next time?
   - **Document Learnings:** Maintaining a journal to document challenges and solutions can help readers build a resource for future reference.

Maintaining Motivation During Tough Times

Motivation can wane during challenging periods, but maintaining it is crucial for continued progress. Here are strategies to help readers stay motivated:

1. **Reconnect with Purpose:**
    - **Reflect on Goals:** Remind readers to revisit their goals and the reasons behind them. Reconnecting with their "why" can reignite their motivation.
    - **Visualize Success:** Encourage readers to visualize their success regularly. Visualization can boost confidence and create a sense of possibility.
2. **Set Small, Achievable Goals:**
    - **Break Down Goals:** Encourage readers to break their larger goals into smaller, manageable tasks. Achieving these small wins can provide a sense of accomplishment and motivation.
    - **Celebrate Progress:** Recognizing and celebrating even minor achievements reinforces positive behavior and keeps motivation high.
3. **Seek Inspiration:**
    - **Role Models:** Share stories of individuals who have overcome challenges and setbacks. Learning about their journeys can inspire readers and provide a sense of solidarity.
    - **Affirmations and Positive Self-Talk:** Encourage readers to practice positive affirmations and self-talk. Reminding themselves of their capabilities can bolster confidence.
4. **Create Accountability:**
    - **Accountability Partners:** Engaging with accountability partners can help maintain motivation.

Regular check-ins with someone who understands the journey can provide encouragement.

- **Join Support Groups:** Joining groups or communities of like-minded individuals fosters a sense of belonging and shared motivation.

Conclusion: Thriving Through Challenges

Challenges and setbacks are inevitable on the journey to transformation, but they do not have to derail progress. By cultivating resilience, developing problem-solving skills, and maintaining motivation, readers can navigate difficult times with confidence and determination.

As you embrace your journey, remember that every challenge is an opportunity for growth. By facing setbacks head-on and viewing them as stepping stones rather than roadblocks, you will not only become a more resilient individual but also inspire others on their journeys. Embrace the challenges, learn from them, and keep moving forward with purpose and

Chapter 7: Celebrating Milestones

The Power of Celebration

In the pursuit of personal and professional growth, it's easy to get caught up in the hustle and bustle of striving toward the next goal. However, pausing to celebrate milestones along the journey is equally important. This chapter explores the significance of recognizing and celebrating achievements, no matter how small, and provides strategies to maintain motivation and inspiration through reflection and acknowledgment of progress. Celebrating milestones not only reinforces positive behavior but also cultivates a sense of fulfillment and purpose, essential for sustained growth.

The Importance of Recognizing Achievements

1. **Psychological Benefits of Celebration:**
   - **Boosting Motivation:** Celebrating achievements serves as a powerful motivator, providing a sense of accomplishment that fuels further efforts. Recognizing progress can help individuals push through challenges and maintain momentum.
   - **Enhancing Well-Being:** Celebrations can improve mental and emotional well-being. Taking time to acknowledge successes fosters positive emotions, reduces stress, and cultivates a more optimistic outlook.
2. **Creating a Positive Feedback Loop:**
   - **Reinforcing Behavior:** When individuals celebrate their milestones, they reinforce the behaviors and actions that led to their achievements. This positive feedback loop encourages continued effort and commitment to their goals.
   - **Building Confidence:** Acknowledging successes, even minor ones, boosts self-confidence and self-esteem. Individuals become more aware of their capabilities, making them more likely to tackle future challenges.
3. **Fostering a Growth Mindset:**
   - **Learning from Progress:** Celebrating milestones encourages individuals to reflect on what they have learned throughout their journey. This reflection enhances a growth mindset, emphasizing the value of learning and adaptability.
   - **Connecting to Purpose:** Celebrations allow individuals to reconnect with their overarching purpose and values. Reflecting on accomplishments

helps clarify the 'why' behind their goals.

Strategies for Celebrating Milestones

1. **Defining Milestones:**
    - **Break Down Goals:** Encourage readers to break their larger goals into smaller, manageable milestones. Clearly defining these milestones allows for more frequent opportunities to celebrate progress.
    - **Establish Criteria for Success:** Readers should establish specific criteria for what constitutes a milestone. This could be reaching a certain percentage of a goal or completing a specific task.
2. **Creating Meaningful Celebrations:**
    - **Personalized Celebrations:** Encourage readers to tailor celebrations to their preferences. Whether it's treating oneself to a favorite meal, a day off, or a small gift, personalizing the celebration enhances its significance.
    - **Sharing Achievements:** Highlight the value of sharing accomplishments with others. Whether through social media, family gatherings, or support groups, sharing milestones can amplify the sense of achievement and inspire others.
3. **Reflective Practices:**
    - **Journaling Achievements:** Encourage readers to maintain a celebration journal where they document milestones, achievements, and reflections on their journey. This practice fosters self-awareness and gratitude.
    - **Creating Vision Boards:** Suggest creating vision

boards that visually represent milestones and achievements. Displaying these boards serves as a constant reminder of progress and encourages further growth.

Maintaining Motivation Through Reflection

1. **Regular Reflection Sessions:**
    - **Scheduled Reflection Time:** Encourage readers to set aside dedicated time for regular reflection. This could be weekly, monthly, or quarterly, depending on personal preference.
    - **Guided Questions:** Provide a list of guided questions to help facilitate reflection, such as:
        - What achievements am I most proud of?
        - What challenges have I overcome to reach these milestones?
        - How have I grown as a person during this journey?
2. **Learning from the Journey:**
    - **Analyzing Progress:** Encourage readers to analyze the progress they've made. Identifying patterns of success and areas for improvement can provide valuable insights for future endeavors.
    - **Acknowledging Setbacks:** Highlight the importance of recognizing setbacks along the way. Readers should reflect on how they overcame challenges and what they learned, reinforcing resilience.
3. **Finding Inspiration:**
    - **Storytelling:** Encourage readers to share their stories of achievements with others. Storytelling fosters connection and can inspire those around them to

pursue their goals.

- **Role Models and Mentors:** Suggest identifying role models or mentors who have successfully navigated similar journeys. Learning from their experiences can provide motivation and inspiration.

Building a Culture of Celebration

1. **Encouraging Celebration in Teams:**
    - **Team Milestones:** For readers working within organizations or teams, celebrating collective achievements is crucial. Encourage team members to recognize and celebrate group milestones together.
    - **Creating a Celebration Ritual:** Suggest establishing a regular celebration ritual within a team or organization, such as monthly meetings to acknowledge progress and achievements.
2. **Creating a Supportive Community:**
    - **Joining or Forming Groups:** Encourage readers to join or form groups focused on personal growth and development. Sharing milestones within a community fosters support and accountability.
    - **Organizing Events:** Readers could consider organizing events to celebrate milestones with like-minded individuals. This could be workshops, retreats, or informal gatherings focused on shared growth.

Conclusion: The Art of Celebration

Celebrating milestones is not just about acknowledging achievements; it's about reinforcing the journey of growth and transformation.

By recognizing and honoring progress, individuals cultivate motivation, boost their confidence, and connect more deeply with their purpose.

As you continue on your journey, remember to pause, reflect, and celebrate the milestones you achieve along the way. Each achievement, no matter how small, contributes to your overall growth and development. Embrace the art of celebration and inspire others to do the same.

Chapter 8: Fostering Continuous Growth

The Journey of Lifelong Learning

In a rapidly changing world, the ability to adapt and evolve is essential for personal and professional success. Continuous growth is not merely a goal but a lifelong commitment to learning, self-improvement, and embracing change. This chapter explores the importance of fostering a mindset of lifelong learning, seeking new opportunities, and embracing the challenges that come with change. By cultivating a culture of continuous growth, individuals can unlock their potential and thrive in an ever-evolving landscape.

The Mindset of Lifelong Learning

1. **Defining Lifelong Learning:**
    - **Continuous Improvement:** Lifelong learning refers to the ongoing, voluntary, and self-motivated pursuit of knowledge for personal or professional development. It encompasses formal education, informal learning, and experiential knowledge gained through life experiences.
    - **Curiosity and Open-Mindedness:** Emphasize the importance of maintaining curiosity and an open mind. Lifelong learners approach new experiences and information with enthusiasm and a desire to understand and grow.
2. **Benefits of a Lifelong Learning Mindset:**
    - **Enhanced Adaptability:** Individuals with a lifelong learning mindset are better equipped to adapt to change. They are more open to new ideas, technologies, and approaches, making it easier to navigate challenges.
    - **Increased Competitiveness:** In the professional landscape, continuous learning ensures individuals remain relevant and competitive. By staying updated on industry trends and skills, they can enhance their employability and career prospects.
    - **Personal Fulfillment:** Lifelong learning contributes to a sense of purpose and fulfillment. Engaging in new experiences and acquiring knowledge can lead to increased satisfaction and happiness in life.

Seeking New Opportunities

1. **Identifying Learning Opportunities:**

- **Formal Education:** Encourage readers to consider enrolling in courses, workshops, or seminars that align with their interests or professional goals. This could include online courses, certifications, or degrees.
- **Informal Learning:** Highlight the value of informal learning experiences, such as reading books, listening to podcasts, or attending community events. These avenues can provide valuable insights and knowledge without the constraints of formal education.

2. **Networking and Collaboration:**
    - **Building Relationships:** Encourage readers to build relationships with individuals from diverse backgrounds and industries. Networking can lead to new opportunities for learning and growth.
    - **Mentorship and Peer Learning:** Suggest seeking mentors or joining peer learning groups. Engaging with others who share similar goals can foster a supportive environment for continuous learning.
3. **Exploring New Interests:**
    - **Diverse Skill Development:** Encourage readers to explore interests outside their current expertise. Engaging in activities such as art, music, sports, or volunteering can provide fresh perspectives and enhance creativity.
    - **Challenging Comfort Zones:** Highlight the importance of stepping outside one's comfort zone. Trying new experiences can lead to personal growth and broaden one's horizons.

Embracing Change

1. **Understanding the Nature of Change:**
    - **Inevitability of Change:** Change is a constant in life, and understanding this reality is crucial. Emphasize that resisting change can hinder growth, while embracing it opens up new possibilities.
    - **Positive Perspective on Change:** Encourage readers to view change as an opportunity for growth rather than a threat. A positive mindset can help individuals navigate transitions more effectively.
2. **Developing Resilience:**
    - **Building Resilience:** Discuss strategies for building resilience in the face of change. This includes developing coping mechanisms, maintaining a support network, and cultivating a positive outlook.
    - **Learning from Failures:** Encourage readers to reframe failures as learning experiences. Analyzing setbacks can provide valuable insights that contribute to future success.
3. **Staying Flexible and Adaptable:**
    - **Cultivating Adaptability:** Highlight the importance of being flexible in one's approach to challenges. Encourage readers to remain open to new ideas and adjust their strategies as needed.
    - **Continuous Self-Assessment:** Suggest regular self-assessment to evaluate personal growth and areas for improvement. This reflective practice can help individuals identify necessary adjustments and stay aligned with their goals.

Continual Evolution

1. **Setting New Goals:**
    - **Goal Reevaluation:** Encourage readers to regularly reevaluate their goals and aspirations. As individuals grow and evolve, their objectives may change, requiring adjustments to their action plans.
    - **Embracing New Challenges:** Highlight the importance of embracing new challenges as opportunities for growth. Taking on projects outside one's comfort zone can lead to skill development and personal advancement.
2. **Investing in Personal Development:**
    - **Seeking Feedback:** Encourage readers to seek constructive feedback from peers, mentors, or coaches. Feedback can provide valuable insights for improvement and help individuals identify blind spots.
    - **Prioritizing Self-Care:** Stress the importance of self-care in the growth journey. Maintaining physical and mental well-being is essential for sustaining motivation and energy for continuous learning.
3. **Creating a Growth-Oriented Environment:**
    - **Surrounding Yourself with Growth-Minded Individuals:** Encourage readers to cultivate relationships with individuals who share a commitment to growth and development. A supportive environment can inspire and motivate continuous improvement.
    - **Emphasizing a Culture of Learning:** For those in leadership roles, emphasize the importance of fostering a culture of learning within teams and organizations. This includes encouraging

experimentation, celebrating learning successes, and supporting ongoing development initiatives.

Conclusion: Your Lifelong Growth Journey

Fostering continuous growth is a lifelong commitment that requires intentionality, curiosity, and resilience. By embracing a mindset of lifelong learning, seeking new opportunities, and adapting to change, individuals can unlock their full potential and navigate the complexities of life with confidence.

As you continue your journey, remember that growth is not a destination but a continuous process. Embrace the challenges and opportunities that come your way, and remain committed to evolving as a person. The path of lifelong learning is one filled with discovery, fulfillment, and endless possibilities.

Afterword: Your Journey as a Catalyst

The Catalyst Within

As we conclude this transformative journey through *Catalyst Unleashed: Revolutionizing Your Journey*, it's essential to reflect on the key concepts we've explored and the empowering tools you've gained. This book has aimed to unlock your potential as a catalyst, enabling you to inspire change in your life and the lives of those around you. By embracing self-discovery, fostering a growth mindset, setting intentional goals, and building meaningful relationships, you are equipped to catalyze transformation in your own journey and in your community.

Key Messages Reinforced

1. **The Power of Self-Discovery:**
    - At the heart of becoming a catalyst is the process of self-discovery. Understanding your values, strengths, and passions is vital to knowing who you are and what impact you want to create. This foundational step lays the groundwork for all future growth.
    - Actionable Step: Take time regularly to reflect on your personal journey. Utilize journaling, meditation, or conversations with trusted friends to gain insights into your evolving self.
2. **Embracing a Transformative Mindset:**
    - Cultivating a transformative mindset is crucial for overcoming challenges and adapting to change. The growth mindset encourages resilience and the belief that abilities can be developed through dedication and hard work.
    - Actionable Step: Identify one limiting belief you hold and challenge it. Replace it with an empowering affirmation that encourages growth and resilience.
3. **Setting Intentional Goals:**
    - Intentional goal-setting aligns your actions with your values and aspirations. By creating a compelling vision for the future, you can channel your energy and resources toward achieving meaningful outcomes.

- Actionable Step: Write down three intentional goals that resonate with your values. Break them into smaller, actionable steps that you can begin implementing immediately.

4. **Building Meaningful Relationships:**
    - The importance of relationships cannot be overstated. Building a supportive network of mentors, peers, and collaborators enhances your growth and opens doors to new opportunities.
    - Actionable Step: Reach out to someone in your network to express gratitude or seek guidance. Take the initiative to foster connections that inspire and empower you.
5. **Taking Decisive Action:**
    - Action is where transformation happens. Moving from intention to execution requires commitment and accountability. Being proactive in your pursuits ensures that you are continually making progress.
    - Actionable Step: Identify one action you've been procrastinating on and commit to completing it within the next week. Break it down into manageable tasks to increase your likelihood of success.
6. **Navigating Challenges and Setbacks:**
    - Challenges are inevitable, but your response to them defines your journey. Embracing resilience and learning from setbacks transforms obstacles into opportunities for growth.
    - Actionable Step: Reflect on a recent challenge you faced. Write down three lessons learned and how they can inform your future actions.
7. **Celebrating Milestones:**
    - Recognition of your achievements, no matter how

small, fuels motivation and encourages ongoing progress. Celebrating milestones cultivates a positive mindset and reinforces your commitment to growth.
- Actionable Step: Create a personal celebration ritual for achieving goals. This could include treating yourself to something special or sharing your achievements with loved ones.

8. **Fostering Continuous Growth:**
   - Lifelong learning and a commitment to continuous growth are essential for sustaining your journey as a catalyst. Embrace new experiences and remain open to evolving in all aspects of your life.
   - Actionable Step: Set aside time each month for personal development. This could involve reading a new book, attending a workshop, or exploring a new hobby.

Empowering You as a Catalyst

You are not merely an observer in your life; you are a catalyst for change. By embracing the tools and strategies discussed in this book, you can ignite transformation within yourself and your community. Your journey as a catalyst begins with you taking intentional steps toward growth, embracing challenges, and inspiring others to do the same.

Actionable Steps for Ongoing Growth

1. **Create a Personal Development Plan:**
   - Outline your goals, the skills you wish to develop, and the resources you need to achieve them. Regularly review and update this plan to ensure you stay aligned with your evolving aspirations.
2. **Join a Community of Catalysts:**
   - Seek out groups or organizations that resonate with

your values and goals. Engage with like-minded individuals who share your passion for growth and transformation.

3. **Engage in Volunteer Work:**
    - Contributing your time and skills to a cause you care about can amplify your impact. Volunteering fosters a sense of purpose and connects you with others who share your commitment to change.
4. **Mentor or Coach Others:**
    - Share your knowledge and experiences with those seeking guidance. Mentoring not only empowers others but also reinforces your own understanding and growth.
5. **Reflect Regularly:**
    - Set aside time for self-reflection. Consider journaling about your experiences, insights, and areas for improvement. This practice can deepen your understanding of your journey and enhance your self-awareness.

Conclusion: Your Ongoing Journey

As you embark on the next phase of your journey, remember that being a catalyst is not a one-time event but a continuous process. Embrace the role of a catalyst with courage and confidence. Allow your journey to inspire those around you, and encourage them to recognize their potential to create positive change.

You possess the power to influence your life and the lives of others profoundly. Embrace your role as a catalyst, and take actionable steps toward creating a future filled with possibility and impact. Your journey is just beginning, and the world is waiting for your unique contributions.

Other Books by this Author

MBBS @ ZERO COST

IS THE DREAM OF BECOMING a doctor being crushed under the weight of ₹1 Crore in private college fees? The thought alone is enough to cause sleepless nights, forcing countless brilliant students and their families to wonder if this noble dream is even possible. You've seen the headlines, you've heard the stories, and now you feel that financial dread firsthand.

This isn't just about money; it's about the years of hard work, the sacrifices made, and the passion to heal—all at risk of being washed away by a tide of crippling debt. You watch as others are forced to compromise, take on life-altering loans, or worse, abandon their medical aspirations altogether. The path to a private MBBS degree can feel like a trap, locking your family's future in a decade-long financial struggle before your career even begins. The agitation is real, and the fear of failure is paralyzing.

But what if there was another way? A proven path to earning your white coat without the soul-crushing financial burden?

Introducing "MBBS @ ZERO COST"—the definitive guide to turning your medical dream into a debt-free reality. This book is the lifeline you've been searching for. It's not about magic; it's a strategic, step-by-step blueprint that demystifies the process of securing a coveted seat in a government medical college. Forget the lakhs and crores. Inside, you'll discover the insider secrets, preparation strategies, and crucial mistakes to avoid that separating the successful few from the rest. Stop agonizing over finances and start building your future. This book is your first, most critical prescription for a successful and affordable medical career. Your dream is possible, and this is how you achieve it.

ALL INDIA INSTITUTE OF MEDICAL SCIENCES: GENERAL KNOWLEDGE (AIIMS Book 1)

Congratulations, future doctor!

You are one step closer to conquering the AIIMS MBBS Entrance Examination.

You hold in your hands the definitive guide to mastering the General Knowledge section of one of India's most competitive medical entrance exams. "ALL INDIA INSTITUTE OF MEDICAL SCIENCES: GENERAL KNOWLEDGE" is meticulously crafted to provide you with the most relevant, well-researched, and up-to-date information necessary to excel.

Authored by Dr. Raam Harvard, this book goes beyond simple facts and figures. It provides a strategic roadmap to understanding the patterns and priorities of the AIIMS exam.

Inside, you will discover:

- Focused Content: Target the exact GK topics and current affairs that frequently appear in the AIIMS exam, saving you valuable preparation time.
- Strategic Insights: Learn how to "Think Like a WINNER" with proven strategies that will give you a competitive edge.
- Expert Guidance: Benefit from the author's intimate secrets and deep understanding of the examination process to avoid common pitfalls.
- A Clear Path to Success: Follow the unique analysis in the second chapter to unlock a study method that can yield returns far greater than the investment in this book.

Stop wasting time on irrelevant material. This guide is your single, most reliable resource to build the confidence and knowledge required to acquire the General Knowledge section. Embrace the mindset of a top-ranked and take the first definitive step toward a successful medical career at AIIMS. What is Psychology?: Mastering the Mind: Unlock the Mysteries, Discover the Insights, Behaviors and Emotions of Your Self, Partners, Relationships, friends, Relations, Competitors, Enemies and Others What is Psychology?: Mastering the Mind: Unlock the Mysteries, Discover the Insights, Behaviors and Emotions of Your Self, Partners, Relationships, friends, Relations, Competitors, Enemies and Other.

DIGITAL Economy Millennium OPPORTUNITY

Are you digitally updated? The revolution is not coming. It is here.

Silently, relentlessly, the digital economy is reshaping our world. But its true potential is not found in the headlines about AI and self-driving cars. It is found in the quiet, monumental shift that is lifting hundreds of millions out of poverty and building the economic superpowers of tomorrow.

DIGITAL Economy Millennium OPPORTUNITY is your guide to understanding this transformation from the front lines. Forget theory—this is the real-world story of how 1.3 billion people are leapfrogging into the future, turning the world's largest democracy into the world's largest digital lab.

With the expert analysis of Aiswarya Ram, MBA, this book dissects the mechanisms of this historic change, exploring:

• Constructive Digital Destruction: How legacy systems of corruption and exclusion were dismantled to make way for a transparent, digitally empowered society.

• Financial Inclusion at Scale: The strategy that ensured the "grass root downtrodden" were the primary beneficiaries of the new digital infrastructure.

• From Liability to Asset: The economic and philosophical shift that occurred when a nation's people became the engine of its digital growth through digitization and demonetization.

This is not just a reference book; it is a call to action. It provides an urgent roadmap for individuals, companies, and countries to adapt, thrive, and lead in the new global landscape. The future belongs to those who understand the forces detailed in these pages.

Digital is the future. Equip yourself for tomorrow, today.

$1000 Billion GOLD POT

UNLOCK THE TRILLION-Dollar Opportunity Hidden in Plain Sight.

What if there was a hidden reservoir of national wealth, a trillion-dollar "Gold Pot" waiting to be claimed by those with the foresight to see it? In a world of economic uncertainty, renowned international finance expert Dr. Raam Harvard reveals the blueprint to one of the most significant wealth creation opportunities of the millennium.

This is the second book in the groundbreaking series that began with DIGITAL Economy Millennium OPPORTUNITY, delving deeper into the mechanisms of national prosperity and financial transformation.

In this concise and potent executive briefing, Dr. Harvard bypasses dense academic theory to deliver a direct, actionable framework for understanding and capitalizing on this emerging economic phenomenon. Drawing on his extensive experience as a leading Corporate Productivity Consultant and faculty for International Financial Reporting Standards (IFRS), he provides an unparalleled insider's view into the forces shaping the future of global finance.

Inside this strategic analysis, you will discover:

- The Anatomy of the "Gold Pot": A clear definition of this $1000 billion opportunity and the macroeconomic conditions that created it.
- The Three Pillars of Growth: Identify the key policy shifts, technological advancements, and industrial sectors poised for exponential growth.
- Strategic Investment Pathways: Understand where capital will flow and how to position yourself or your organization to benefit from this massive economic shift.
- Global Implications: Explore the ripple effects of this wealth creation event on international trade, investment, and monetary policy.
- A Roadmap for the Future: Gain the critical insights needed to navigate the new financial landscape, from the rise of digital currencies to the restructuring of traditional industries.

This is more than a book; it is a strategic advantage. It is for the investor seeking the next frontier, the policymaker shaping a nation's future, and the entrepreneur building the next global enterprise. Knowledge within these pages is the key to unlocking a new era of prosperity.

The opportunity of a millennium is here. Secure your strategic advantage today.

Demonetization - the QUANTUM JUMP

IMAGINE A SINGLE GOVERNMENT decision rendering 86% of a nation's currency obsolete overnight. Was it a reckless gambling or a calculated leap into the future? Demonetization the QUANTUM JUMP argues it was the latter—a revolutionary catalyst that forever changed India's financial DNA.

This comprehensive analysis moves beyond the immediate shockwaves to reveal the long-term strategic thinking behind one of the most audacious economic experiments in modern history. Journey from the ancient Vedic system of currency to the future of a cashless "E-Life," and uncover the hidden architecture of this global phenomenon. The book dissects the legacy systems of black money, tax evasion, and real estate that the "Quantum Jump" was designed to disrupt, offering a clear-eyed look at the policy's consequences—the good, the bad, and the ugly.

Through insightful analysis and compelling stories, you will connect the dots of India's new economy and understand the profound structural shifts that are now underway. This is not just a book about a single policy; it is a guide to understanding revolutionary economic change, the future of money, and the bold vision shaping the world's largest democracy. Are you ready to grasp the full impact of the world's most disruptive financial shift?

DEMONETISATION: SUCCESS or FAILURE?

On the night of 8 November 2016, India witnessed a monetary shock of unprecedented scale. In a televised address, Prime Minister

Narendra Modi announced that with just four hours' notice, the nation's two largest currency denominations—the 500- and 1,000-rupee notes—would be rendered worthless. This single act invalidated 86% of the cash in circulation, triggering a seismic event that brought the world's largest democracy to a virtual standstill.

Was this a masterstroke against corruption or a monumental mismanagement of the economy? DEMONETISATION: SUCCESS or FAILURE? provides the definitive, balanced analysis of one of modern India's most audacious and controversial policies.

The government's objectives were ambitious and, over time, evolved significantly. This book meticulously dissects each stated goal against the hard evidence, revealing a complex and often contradictory legacy:

• The War on Black Money: The primary stated goal was to unearth vast troves of illicit, untaxed cash and destroy counterfeit currency used to finance terrorism. Yet, the policy's effectiveness was immediately questioned when a staggering 99.3% of the demonetized currency was returned to the banking system, prompting many economists to declare this core objective a failure. This book examines why the initial assumptions about black money—that it is primarily held in cash—were flawed from the start.

• The Digital Revolution: As the initial narrative faltered, the focus shifted to transforming India into a "cashless" or "less-cash" society. This book quantifies the undeniable success of this secondary objective, detailing the explosive growth in digital payments, the widespread adoption of the Unified Payments Interface (UPI), and the significant push toward the formalization of the economy.

• Expanding the Tax Base: Proponents point to a tangible increase in tax compliance, with the number of income tax returns filed growing by 24.7% in the year following demonetization. The analysis explores whether this expansion was a direct and sustainable result of the policy or a temporary outcome of forcing cash into formal channels.

While some hailed these outcomes as long-term victories, they came at a tremendous cost. The book provides a sober assessment of the policy's severe and far-reaching consequences:

• The Economic Shockwave: The sudden liquidity crunch triggered a sharp contraction in economic activity. This analysis delves into the quantitative data, exploring estimates from the Economic Survey and prominent economists who projected a decline in GDP growth ranging from 0.25% to as high as 2%. The book investigates the slowdown in key sectors like manufacturing, real estate, and construction, providing a clear picture of the macroeconomic damage.

• The Human Cost: Beyond the macroeconomic data lies a story of immense human hardship. The policy disproportionately impacted the cash-reliant informal sector, which employs over 85% of India's workforce. This book gives voice to the daily wage laborers, small farmers, and micro-entrepreneurs who faced devastating losses of income and employment, with some estimates suggesting 1.5 million jobs were lost in the immediate aftermath.

• The Great Intellectual Divide: The policy ignited a fierce debate among the world's leading economic minds. This book navigates the dissenting views of Nobel laureate Amartya Sen, who called it a "despotic act," and former central bank governor Raghuram Rajan, who warned of the costs, contrasting them with the supportive arguments of economists like Jagdish Bhagwati, who hailed it as a "courageous reform".

DEMONETISATION: SUCCESS or FAILURE? moves beyond partisan rhetoric to deliver a data-driven, nuanced verdict. It unpacks the complex interplay of economics and politics, answering the crucial question that continues to haunt policymakers and citizens alike: How do we measure the true legacy of a policy that was, for many, an economic disaster but was simultaneously perceived as a political masterstroke? This book is an essential resource for anyone seeking to understand this pivotal moment in India's history.

BITCOIN SECRETS

Unlock the Power of Bitcoin: Your Guide to Navigating the Future of Money is Here.

Feeling left behind by the Bitcoin revolution? Are you overwhelmed by technical terms, conflicting advice, and the fear of making a costly mistake? You're not alone. The world of cryptocurrency can seem like an exclusive club, but "BITCOIN SECRETS" is your personal invitation to join with confidence.

This is not just another book about what Bitcoin is. This is a practical, step-by-step guide on what to do. Forget the get-rich-quick hype. This book provides the foundational knowledge and actionable strategies you need to treat Bitcoin as a serious technological and financial tool.

Inside "BITCOIN SECRETS," you will discover:

• The Core Secrets of the Blockchain: Understand in simple, plain English how the technology works and why it's poised to change everything.

• The Smart Way to Buy & Sell: A step-by-step walkthrough of acquiring your first Bitcoin, avoiding high fees, and choosing the right exchanges.

• Fort Knox Security Protocols: Learn the crucial secrets to securing your digital assets. We cover cold storage, hardware wallets, and the common pitfalls that leave others vulnerable.

• Decoding the Market: Uncover the patterns behind market cycles, understand the impact of "halving," and learn to separate genuine trends from market noise.

• Beyond Bitcoin: A clear overview of how Bitcoin's success has paved the way for thousands of other cryptocurrencies and the wider world of DeFi (Decentralized Finance).

• Common Mistakes and How to Avoid Them: Learn from the errors of others to protect your time, money, and peace of mind.

Whether you're a complete beginner who has never bought a single satoshi, or you've dabbled in crypto and wanted to deepen your understanding, "BITCOIN SECRETS" is the clear, concise, and indispensable resource you've been searching for.

Don't just watch the future of finance unfolded a part of it. Scroll up and unlock the secrets today!

BUY BITCOIN with CREDIT CARD

Ready to finally own your first Bitcoin but overwhelmed by the complexity? You're not alone.

The world of cryptocurrency can feel like an exclusive club, filled with technical jargon and confusing platforms. Many potential investors feel left behind, worried about making a costly mistake. But what if there was a simple, familiar way to get started in minutes?

In "BUY BITCOIN with CREDIT CARD," you'll discover the most straightforward path to entering the digital asset market. This book demystifies the entire process, cutting through the noise to provide a clear, secure, and easy-to-follow roadmap. It's designed specifically for the absolute beginner who wants to act now, using a tool they already have in their wallet.

Inside this essential guide, you will learn:

• Step-by-Step Walkthroughs: Clear, illustrated instructions on how to purchase Bitcoin from reputable platforms using your credit card.

• Choosing the Right Exchange: A breakdown of the best and safest platforms that accept credit card payments, comparing their pros and cons.

• Navigating Fees and Limits: Understand exactly what you'll pay and how to minimize costs, so there are no surprises.

• Security First: Crucial tips on how to secure your new digital assets immediately after purchase to protect them from hackers and theft.

• Common Pitfalls to Avoid: Learn from the mistakes of others so you can invest with confidence and avoid rookie errors.

• What to Do Next: A brief introduction to crypto wallets and what your options are after you've made your first purchase.

This book is not for crypto experts. It's for the everyday person—the student, the professional, the retiree—who is curious about Bitcoin and wants a safe, simple, and immediate way to get started.

Don't let confusion be the barrier to your financial future. Scroll up to begin your crypto journey today!

Don't miss out!

Visit the website below and you can sign up to receive emails whenever Dr.Raam Harvard publishes a new book. There's no charge and no obligation.

https://books2read.com/r/B-A-OLZW-MSVWG

Connecting independent readers to independent writers.

Did you love *The Potential Trap*? Then you should read *The 7-Figure Network*[1] by Dr.Raam Harvard!

[2]

Feeling invisible in your industry, stuck on a career plateau while others with less experience climb the ladder? It's not about working harder—it's about connecting smarter. This book reveals the one secret connection strategy that turns overlooked professionals into sought-after industry leaders in just 90 days.

Inside this 9-chapter guide, you will **discover how to:**

Master a proven, step-by-step system for career development and unlock rapid professional growth.Develop unshakable executive presence and ***gain the influence*** to command respect in any room.Transform networking from a source of anxiety into an ***authentic strategy*** for building genuine, high-value connections.Unlock the

1. https://books2read.com/u/38pMxr
2. https://books2read.com/u/38pMxr

personal branding secrets that fast track your career and open doors to 7-figure opportunities.

Forget collecting business cards. This book unveils a powerful 90-day framework for strategic relationship building. You'll learn a repeatable process designed to create a powerful, supportive ecosystem that generates opportunities, drives revenue, and builds a legacy—not just a contact list.

Perfect for ambitious professionals, entrepreneurs, sales leaders, and anyone ready to stop being ordinary and start building their 7-figure network.

Read more at https://drraam.com/.

Also by Dr.Raam Harvard

Money

Demonetization the QUANTUM JUMP
DIGITAL Economy Millennium OPPORTUNITY

Psychology

What is Psychology?: Unlocking Practical Tools for Growth
The 7-Figure Network
The Potential Trap

Watch for more at https://drraam.com/.

About the Author

Dr. Raam Harvard is a well-known author.

His published books include MBBS @ ZERO COST, All India Institute Of Medical Sciences, DIGITAL Economy Millennium OPPORTUNITY, $1000 Billion GOLD POT, Demonetization the QUANTUM JUMP, Demonetisation: SUCCESS or FAILURE?, BITCOIN SECRETS , BUY BITCOIN with CREDIT CARD, etc.

He was bestowed with the International Business Excellence Award and the Best Entrepreneur Award.

Dr. Raam Harvard is faculty for International Financial Reporting Standards (IFRS), International Accounting & Auditing Standards (IAAS), Fraud &Forensic Audit, COBIT standard, ISO standard, Corporate Finance Taxation, Foreign Trade, Information Technology Audit, Java Programming, Oracle, Valuation of assets, Audit of Public Sector Undertakings, and Public-Private Partnerships.

He is a leading Corporate Productivity Consultant (TopmostConsultants.com) specialized in Corporate Training for Productivity improvement/Scaling-up and development of wealth of individuals and organizations.

He is also Professional Member of International Solar Energy Society, International Expert Network (IEN), Patron- Builders Association of India, Fellow- Solar Energy Society of India, and Life Fellow- Professional Counseling Psychologists Association.

He serves as Chairman of M/s V V I P Wealth Advisors Worldwide a Triple ISO accredited Organization and the Poverty Eradication Charitable Trust(Triple ISO).

He is an honorable member of Gemological Institute of America (GIA), Federation of Exporters Organization (FIEO), Gem & Jewelry Export Promotion Council, Gem &Jewelry Federation, Confederation of Indian Industry, Environment Council and several other reputed organizations.

He is Guest Faculty for International students.

Ms. Aiswarya Ram, a Model , and winner of Best Women Entrepreneur Award, with MBA in Information Systems, published research papers in **International Journal of Commerce and Innovations**, co-authors several books, including Demonetization_the QUANTUM JUMP, DIGITAL Economy Millennium OPPORTUNITY, etc.

She services as honorary secretary to the triple ISO accredited Poverty Eradication Charitable Trust. Her efforts in women emancipation programs contributed the main thread.

RunToTOP.com

Read more at https://drraam.com/.

About the Publisher

"**Knowledge is the most powerful tool for change.**" — Dr. Raam Harvard

Poverty Eradication Trust (Triple ISO)

Impact Publishing with a Purpose. Certified. Trusted. Triple ISO Standard.

Welcome to the powerhouse behind this book — **Poverty Eradication Trust (PET)** — where words don't just entertain, they **ignite minds, uplift lives, and spark real change.**

We're not your regular publishing house.We are **a purpose-driven, globally certified Triple ISO organization**, built on a mission:**Educate.Empower.Eradicate Poverty.**

Where Stories Change Lives We believe in the power of stories to transform hearts, minds—and the world! We're not just about creating unforgettable books; we're on a mission to eradicate poverty, one page at a time.

A Legacy of Impact Founded with a vision to blend literary excellence with social good, we pour our heart into every story we publish. From pulse-pounding thrillers to soul-stirring romances, our books are crafted to captivate, inspire, and leave you craving more. But that's not all—every purchase you make supports our initiatives to uplift communities, fund education, and break the cycle of poverty worldwide.

Why Readers Love Us Readers adore our curated collection of viral, unputdownable stories that keep them up all night. You can trust that every book meets the highest standards of quality, sustainability, and ethical impact. Join a global community of book lovers who are making a difference.

What We Publish

From **gripping fiction thrillers** that race your pulse, to **mind-shifting non-fiction** and **life-transforming educational content**, we craft and curate content that hits hard, sticks deep, and **sells worldwide.**

We're behind:

50+ Fiction Thrillers20+ Non-Fiction Game-Changers80+ Online Psychology CoursesSeries on AI, Cybersecurity, Bitcoin, and more!

All designed to **educate, entertain, and empower**.

Who We Serve

We don't just cater to readers — we serve:**Entrepreneurs & Students** looking to learn smarter.**Thriller Fans** who crave adrenaline and intrigue.**Corporates** seeking psychological edge through our consulting and content.

Where to Find Us

Fiction & Thrillers: Online Courses: Consulting Services: Author Branding & Books:

Join the Movement

We're more than a publisher — we're a **revolution** in storytelling and psychology-led transformation.

Follow us to discover our latest releases, behind-the-scenes magic, and the incredible impact your support creates. Share your reading journey with #PETBooks and let's spark a revolution—because great stories can change the world, and together, we're creating a brighter future!

Be part of our tribe:

Poverty Eradication Trust

Triple ISO Certified | Impact Driven | Story Powered*"Because books should do more than sit on shelves — they should build futures."*

Thank You for Reading with Purpose!

9 789349 611979

Printed at Repro India Ltd.